Where Does It Come From?

From Wheat to Bread

by Penelope S. Nelson

T0014941

Bullfrog Books

Ideas for Parents and Teachers

Bullfrog Books let children practice reading informational text at the earliest reading levels. Repetition, familiar words, and photo labels support early readers.

Before Reading

- Discuss the cover photo. What does it tell them?
- Look at the picture glossary together. Read and discuss the words.

Read the Book

- "Walk" through the book and look at the photos. Let the child ask questions. Point out the photo labels.
- Read the book to the child, or have him or her read independently.

After Reading

- Prompt the child to think more. Ask: Wheat grows in fields. Can you name other plants that grow in fields?

Bullfrog Books are published by Jump!
5357 Penn Avenue South
Minneapolis, MN 55419
www.jumplibrary.com

Copyright © 2021 Jump! International copyright reserved in all countries. No part of this book may be reproduced in any form without written permission from the publisher.

Library of Congress Cataloging-in-Publication Data

Names: Nelson, Penelope, 1994– author.
Title: From wheat to bread / Penelope S. Nelson.
Description: Minneapolis: Jump!, Inc., [2021]
Series: Where does it come from?
Audience: Ages 5–8.
Audience: Grades K–1.
Identifiers: LCCN 2019053378 (print)
LCCN 2019053379 (ebook)
ISBN 9781645275442 (library binding)
ISBN 9781645275459 (paperback)
ISBN 9781645275466 (ebook)
Subjects: LCSH: Bread—Juvenile literature.
Wheat—Juvenile literature.
Classification: LCC TX769 .N45 2021 (print)
LCC TX769 (ebook) | DDC 641.81/5—dc23
LC record available at https://lccn.loc.gov/2019053378
LC ebook record available at https://lccn.loc.gov/2019053379

Editor: Jenna Gleisner
Designer: Anna Peterson

Photo Credits: SeDmi/Shutterstock, cover; monticello/Shutterstock, 1; cristi1801804/Shutterstock, 3; StockImageFactory.com/Shutterstock, 4; Ievgenii Meyer/Shutterstock, 5, 22tl, 23tm; smereka/Shutterstock, 6–7, 22tr, 23bl; Istvan Csak/Shutterstock, 7, 23bm; Juliastilz/Shutterstock, 8–9, 22mr, 23tr; Michelle Lee Photography/Shutterstock, 10–11, 22br, 23br; Iakov Filimonov/Shutterstock, 12, 16, 22bl; Rimma Bondarenko/Shutterstock, 13 (background); Jiri Hera/Shutterstock, 13 (foreground); Shutterstock, 14–15, 23tl; JackF/Adobe Stock, 17; CandyBox Images/Shutterstock, 18–19, 22ml; whyframestudio/iStock, 20–21; Preto Perola/Shutterstock, 24.

Printed in the United States of America at Corporate Graphics in North Mankato, Minnesota.

Table of Contents

From Flour 4

From Wheat to Table 22

Picture Glossary 23

Index 24

To Learn More 24

Mel loves bread!

Where does it come from?

wheat

Wheat!
It grows in fields.

Farmers harvest it.
Then it goes to a mill.

mill

Machines grind it into flour.

flour

salt

yeast

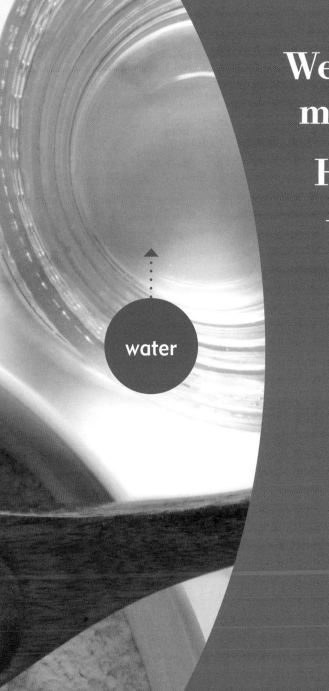

water

We use flour to make bread.

How?

We add water, salt, and yeast.

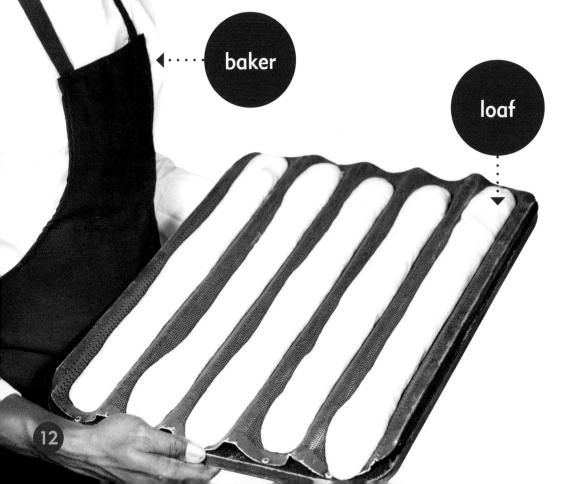

Bakers make loaves. Some are long.

baker

loaf

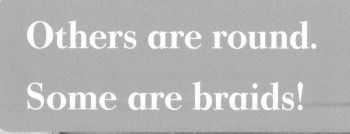

braid

Others are round.
Some are braids!

dough

Dough rises.
This takes time.

Time to bake!
Dough goes in ovens.

Perfect!

We buy it.
Yum!

Do you like bread?

From Wheat to Table

How does bread get to our tables?

1. Wheat grows in fields.

2. Farmers harvest wheat.

3. Wheat is ground into flour at mills.

4. Bakers add ingredients to flour to make dough.

5. Dough bakes in ovens.

6. We buy and eat bread!

Picture Glossary

dough
A thick mixture of mainly flour and water that is used to make bread.

fields
Pieces of open land, sometimes used for growing crops.

grind
To crush something into small pieces or powder.

harvest
To gather crops from a field.

mill
A building with machines that grind grain into flour.

yeast
A fungus used to make bread dough rise.

Index

bake 16

bakers 12

dough 15, 16

farmers 7

flour 8, 11

loaves 12

mill 7

ovens 16

salt 11

water 11

wheat 5

yeast 11

To Learn More

Finding more information is as easy as 1, 2, 3.

❶ Go to www.factsurfer.com

❷ Enter "fromwheattobread" into the search box.

❸ Choose your book to see a list of websites.